MW00789152

Yiayia Approved

Greek Sayings, Proverbs, Advice, Superstitions, & More…

Angela Vardalos Saclamacis

Copyright © 2021 Angela Saclamacis. All rights
reserved. No part of this publication may be
reproduced, distributed, or transmitted in any form or
by any means, including photocopying, recording, or
other electronic or mechanical methods, without the
prior written permission of the publisher, except in
case of brief quotations embodied in critical reviews
and certain other non-commercial uses permitted by
copyright law.

For permission requests, or general enquiries email:
angevardalos@gmail.com

ISBN: 978-1-7779755-4-8 (eBook)
ISBN: 978-1-7779755-3-1 (Paperback)

First edition, 2022

This book is dedicated to my wonderful and supportive husband Jim, and daughters, my parents Sophie and Peter Vardalos, in-laws Evangelia and Gavriil Saclamacis—all who have been loving, wise, and full of advice, along with adding so much laughter in my life!

Huge thanks to my contributors and cheerleading squads in "trans-creating", including Elina Zanakis Vardalos who has been by my side since the start of this idea, and my in-laws for their countless hours of help.

3

Yiayia Approved

Introduction

In 1988, I was planning to marry my best friend in the dead of winter in Winnipeg, Manitoba, Canada. A huge Greek wedding is always exciting! But, what I didn't expect were the strong objections to getting married in a Greek Orthodox Church during a leap year... in February... and on an even, double-digit year!

After many calls and visits with our wonderful priest, we were finally given a blessing to proceed with the wedding. To this day we are happily married!

Throughout my life, my parents, grandparents, aunts, uncles, in-laws and so many others, have given me "advice". Most were dismissed with a chuckle. Some were respected, especially those that are based on religion. While others made me completely puzzled and perplexed.

However, some are engrained in our genetic DNA that make us not only follow them, but will likely be the reason they continue to be passed along to the next generation, and beyond.

Growing up, I would always ask questions and wondered the meaning of different sayings. I was constantly amazed at the variety of expressions throughout Greece, and in other parts of the world where Greeks reside.

Hearing "*FTOO, FTOO, FTOO*" isn't something odd to anyone growing up in a Greek world, and has likely been heard since a young age! Spitting three times, symbolizing the Holy Trinity, while also wearing jewellery of the "*máti*" or "evil eye", is a sure way to diminish any form of evil energy or presence. This is especially after giving or receiving a compliment.

Prayers to rid others of *máti* is a blessing that is taught, passed down, and called upon for those that suspect they have been cursed with feelings of dizziness, anxiety, light-headedness and with light flu-like symptoms.

A quick phone call to Yiayia, asking her to do *Vaskanía* or the "*máti* prayer" would rid all the nasty symptoms, even if she was on the other side of the world!

We would know when dad was calling the *horió* (village) to speak with Yiayia, and Pappou, living in Drimos, Greece. It was always super early on a weekend morning and he always yelled thinking that he had to speak louder since they were so far away!

Whenever the line wasn't clear, or they couldn't hear my dad, he would do his infamous "Greek shepherd's whistle". I'm certain our neighbours could hear him too!

I remember hearing roosters and pigs in the background of the *kafenío* (café), where the only village phone was located when speaking with my grandparents.

Kids today are blessed with being able to video call whenever they want to see and speak with their grandparents, and they look in disbelief when we share these stories from growing up in a Greek home!

Some kids today have never even seen a pomegranate in its full form, as Yiayia would always have them peeled, with the bright red seeds and arils in a bowl, ready to snack on.

I only recently learned about pomegranates being smashed on New Year's eve, and that a baby tooth is thrown onto the roofs of homes while saying a rhyme that asks for a crow to carry it away and bring back another that will be strong.

With these new learnings, it dawned on me that I really didn't know much at all about my Greek heritage and culture, despite growing up with all these "Yiayia-isms"!

So, in my research, I came to realize that these celebrations and sayings can all be documented in one place. Initially, I thought I'd have a few pages that could be fun to share with friends. But in no time they became chapters, so I decided to gather them all here.

So, within these pages, you will see some sayings and superstitions I learned. Some are only in English. For those in Greek, I have sounded out each word to the best of my ability into English as I believe one would say it—or as "Greek-lish".

Kindly note that "d's" are almost always pronounced as a hard "th", and for the Greek letter X (not to be confused with the English letter "x"), it's pronounced as "he".

I don't claim to be an expert, and many of these may not be "trans-created" 100% correctly. "Lost in translation" does happen, depending on who is reading and where they are from.

However, my hope is that by sharing these light-hearted findings, that you will get a chuckle from some, while learning a few new ones too!

I now have an even greater appreciation of our proud Greek heritage!

CHAPTER 1
~ Out-and-About ~

Ta mátia téssera - Likely the most commonly known saying. It suggests that one keep watch with, or have four eyes!

Ta mátia dekatéssera - an amplified version of the above, of watching with 14 eyes… since having just four eyes is never enough!

΄E kalí eméra fenete apo to proé – means that you can tell in the morning that it's going to be a good day!

Kállio argá pará poté – means better late than never.

΄Opou ypárhei kapnós ypárhei kai fotiá – means where there is smoke, there is fire.

Vadízo argá yiatí viásome - means that I'm walking slow because I'm in a hurry.

Ópoíos viázetai skondáfti – means that when you're in a hurry, everything goes wrong. Lose your balance and you fall down. So, take things easy and don't rush. Think things through.

Tis nýchtas ta kamómata, ta vlépei eméra kai gelá - means that the day sees the night's shenanigans and laughs.

Ópoíos tin nýchta perpatáei, láspes kai skatá patáei – means that whoever walks at night, steps in mud and *poop*.

Tha sou ponésoun ta lemá - translates that 'your neck is always turning around to see what's going on', meaning that you are sticking your nose in other people's business.

Prágmata pou den se andiaféroun min ta rotás – translates to 'you don't need to ask for things that are none of your business'.

Sikóthikan ta pódia na diatáxon to kefáli - means to stand up on your feet so you can think more clearly.

E tsépi tou éhi kavoúria yia kápoion polí tsingoúni - translates to 'his pocket has crabs in it', sarcastically meaning he is cheap and can't reach into his wallet to pay, or he'll be pinched by a crab.

Ópoíos éhi mýges mygiázetai - translates to 'whoever has flies on them gets bothered', meaning that whoever is guilty will feel it.

Dáskale pou dídaskes kai nómo den ekráteises - means that the teacher taught but doesn't follow the rules.

Katharós ouranós astrapés den fovátai - translates to 'the clear sky is not afraid of lightning', meaning with good conscience there is nothing to worry about.

Mia tou kléfti, dyo tou kléfti, treis kai ton tsakósame! - means that you can cheat once, you can cheat twice, but you will eventually get caught!

Min háneis tin eméra sou yia tin nýchta – means do not waste your day for the night.

Vréhei kareklopódara - translates to 'it's raining chair legs', but means that it's raining hard, or 'cats and dogs'.

Me to kaló pódi próta - translates to 'use the good foot first'. This suggests that we always enter a plane, building, or house with the right foot first!

Káthe embódio yia kaló – means that every obstacle is for the good.

Voutá tin glóssa sou sto myaló sou - means to think before you speak.

Kráta me na se krató, na anevoúme sto vounó - translates to 'hold me while I hold you, so we can climb the mountain', meaning let's help each other accomplish challenges together.

Treis laloún kai dyo horévoun - translates to 'three are singing and two are dancing', but means that they have lost their minds and you don't agree with them.

Kiss your *stavró* (cross) before it's put on.

One Greek alone can conquer the world, put two Greeks together and there will be a war, and put three Greeks together—they will build a church!
Submitted by; Paul Lambrakis Seal Beach, CA On behalf of; Father George Stephanides ~ of blessed memory! ~ Pastor, St. Paul's Greek Orthodox Church, Irvine, California.

Trellós pappás se váftise - translates to 'the crazy priest baptized you', but means that you say something unbelievable.

To polí to kérie eléison, to variéte kai o pappás – translates to 'even the priest is getting tired of hearing *lord give mercy to me*', but means you're bragging too much, and I'm tired of hearing it over and over.

Keranovólos érotas - passionately in love.

New Year's Eve - when the clock strikes midnight, a pomegranate is rolled and smacked on the front door of the house. The more seeds that scatter on the ground, the luckier the New Year will be.

Mártis – a celebration of spring. Handmade wristbands are worn during the month of March, made of white and red thread. In modern times, decorative beads have been added. At the end of March, they are taken off and tied to trees (without the decorations and beads) so birds can use for their nests.

Ena helithóni den férni tin ánixi - a swallow does not bring spring. Or, that a single effort or person does not always succeed.

Botides - On the Holy Saturday in Corfu, an annual custom combines Orthodox customs and Venetian traditions where residents in the heart of the old town push red ceramic pots filled with red ribbons and water off balconies. It is to symbolize pushing the evil spirit from the island and celebrates the first Resurrection of Christ.

After Easter service, many make the sign of the cross with the lit candle from church above their front door.

Kai sta dekά sou - you'll hear this often at bridal showers and weddings, said to those not married and translates to "and to yours". It is a well-wishing for their future wedding.

Kai sta pedíon - is similar to "kai sta dika sou" as it's a well-wishing that is said to those who are married, and is for their children's future wedding.

Aftos eínai diprósopos – means that, 'he is two-faced'.

΄Οpoíos éxo apó to horo, polla potámi údia xérei - translates to 'anyone outside of the dance who knows a lot of songs', but means that 'although one is giving advice, they may not know the situation'.

΄Οla ta dáktyla den eínai ta edia allá mazí léne mia prosefhí - not all fingers are the same but when they come together they say a prayer.

CHAPTER 2
~ Homefront ~

Kýlise o téntzeris kai vríke to kapáki - translates to 'the pot rolled over and found the lid', but means that they both fit together perfectly.

Ópoíos kaígetai sto hyló, fysá kai to yiaoúrti - translates to 'whoever burns their mouth on porridge will then be so cautious that they will blow on their yogurt', meaning that once you've been burned once, you will be careful the next time.

Tha fás kai thá horépsis - translates to 'not only are you going to eat, but you are going to dance too'.
Submitted by; Paul Lambrakis, Seal Beach, CA
On behalf of; Yiayia "Dr. Olympia"

Tha to fás kai thá pis kai ena tragoúdi – translates to 'not only are you going to eat, but you are going to sing a song too'!

Poté min tragoudáte ótan tróte. Tha pantrefteís énan tsigáno - translates to 'never sing when you eat. You'll marry a nomad traveller'.

Spoudéa ta láhana - translates to 'cabbages are great', but means you don't agree with the gossip you're hearing.

Sigá to polyéleo - translates to 'slow down the chandelier', but means that someone is telling you something you don't believe, or it is of little value.

Sikóthikan ta agoúria na díroune ton manávi - translates to 'the cucumbers rose up to hit the grocer', and means those that are ignorant have come to replace experts!

Spiti mou, spitáki mou kai ftoho-kalyvaki mou – translates to 'it's better to live in my little house, even if it is poor'! Meaning that I'm happy to live in this house that I love, even if it's not large, modern, or fancy.

To kaló erótima - means 'you're asking a good question'!

'Opoíos den thélei na zemósi déka méres koskínizi – means that someone is lazy to do work so will always find millions of excuses!

Mou psíneis to psári sta heíli - translates to 'you cook the fish on my lips', but means that you're grilling me, yapping, being mean and making everyone's life difficult.

Ton fronímon ta pediá prin peinásoun mageirévoun - means that the wise children cook before they are hungry.

Kátse sta avgá sou – translates to 'sit on your eggs', and means just stay put like a chicken! Or, don't interfere… do nothing.

Stou koufoú ti pórta, óso théleis vrónta - means that you can knock on a deaf man's door forever. Or, don't waste your time on those not interested in listening.

'O kalós o noikokýris xérei kai állo monopáti – means that the good housekeeper always knows another path. Or, a clever person finds another way.

Kápiou tou harízane ena gáitharo, kai aftos ton ky'taze sta dóntia – translates to 'they were giving someone a donkey as a gift and he was more concerned about his teeth' and means he was super fussy and not grateful for the gift!

Ópou kratá, kalá krateí ki ópou éhase as gyrévei - means the one who has it holds it tight, but the one who lost it is searching.

Tha sou dóso to "passapórt" sou– translates to 'I'm giving you your passport', but means I'm kicking you out of the house!

Ópos éstroses tha kemitheís - translates to 'where he lays down, he will sleep', but means when someone is talking about investing in something that you don't agree with, you tell them it's their choice as actions have consequences. Or, that your preparation influences your results.

Fasoúli, fasoúli gemízei to sakoúli - translates to 'bean by bean, the bag fills', and means that every little bit counts.

Opoíos anakatévetai me to pítouro, ton tróne e kótes - translates to 'whoever mixes with the bran is eaten by the chickens', but means don't mess in someone else's business and don't gossip.

Gáta pou koimátai, pontikoús den piánei - means that a sleeping cat catches no mice, or a person does not succeed.

Mazí me ton vasilikó potízete kai e glástra - translates to 'watering the basil waters the pot too', but means that with the good ones, there are always bad ones too. Or, collateral benefit.

Geia sas kai e skoúpa brostá sas - is said when you welcome someone into your home but the broom is by the front door. Even if you spent the entire day cleaning and sweeping, you've ruined their first impression.

Kai tou bogiatzí o kópanos - translates to 'and the painter's baton', but means you keep repeating the same story and don't make any sense with what you're saying.

Ta louloúdia me ta louloúdia! - translates to 'flowers with flowers', and means that good people will be with good people, and bad will be with bad.

Kounioúntai ta sideriká kounioúntai kai e velónes - translates to 'the irons and the sewing needles are shaking', but means that when you see someone else doing something (exercising, dancing, or buying something expensive), you want to do it or have it too. But you can't because of your age, or ability. It's said with a bit of jealousy.

'Otan leípei e gáta, horévoun ta pondíkia - when the cat is away, the mice dance. Or, when the boss is away the workers misbehave.

Na skáso e na kláso – translates to 'do you want me to shut up or pass gas', but means, 'do you want me to keep quiet or tell lies'.

'Oti akoús stin geitoniá sou periménete stin goniá sou - translates to 'whatever you hear in your neighbourhood, just stay in your corner', and means to ignore it.

Mia trýpa sto neró - translates to 'a hole in the water', but means that you're not doing it properly, so nothing will be achieved.

Egó diatázo to gáidaro kai o gáidaros diatázei tin ourá tou - translates to, 'I order my donkey to do something and he orders his tail to do it'. It means, as an example, when you ask your kids to do something, and they ask their brother/sister to do it instead.

Mazí me to skató pai kai to ftiári - translates to 'when you throw away the *poop*, you also throw away the shovel', meaning when you don't care for someone as they're full of *poop*.

To mílo péfti káto apo tin mília – translates to the apple doesn't fall far from the tree.

Bros sta káli, ti éhei o pónos - means we will do anything for beauty, even if it hurts.

Kólos kai vrakí - translates to your 'butt and panties' but means, maybe with jealousy… that they're inseparable or matching.

Min petágesai san tin pordí sto vrakí - translates to 'don't jump like a fart in your underwear', but means when you get interrupted by someone, you ask them to mind their own business.

Na mou trýpíseis ti mytí mou - translates to 'pierce my nose', but means when you try to tell someone something but they don't want to believe you—you're trying to explain that you're telling the truth.

´Eheis glóssa psalídi - translates to 'your tongue is like scissors', but means you're talking too much. Like scissors cut all the time, you're taking too much all the time.

´E siopí mou pros apándisi sou – my silence is your answer.

´E glóssa kókala den éhei kai kókala tsakízei – means the tongue doesn't have bones but breaks bones—catastrophe from gossip.

Píres polý aéra - means you're full of hot air.

Dóse thárros tou horiáti kai tha aneví kai sto kreváti – means that when you trust or encourage someone too much, they'll take advantage or abuse you in many ways.

Pírame ta mátia mas kai fýgame - translates to 'we took our eyes and left', but means that we had no choice but to leave, with a broken heart seeking a better life.

To éna héri pléni to állo kai ta dyo to prósopo – translates to, 'one hand washes the other, but together they wash the face'.

Mou éprixes to sykóti mou - translates to 'my liver swelled', but means I'm tired of hearing the same story over and over again.

Gelái kalýtera opoíos gelái teleftaíos - means that you laugh better when you're the last one laughing.

Alla akoúei e theía mou ke álla akoún ta aftiá mou - translates to 'my aunt hears the story a different way than my ears do', but means that I hear and understand the story differently than what you're telling me.

Egó geló me dódeka kai déka tris me ména – translates to 'I laugh 12 or 13 times', but means that I'm not really sure that I know what I'm doing.

Sterní mou gnósi, na s´eíha próta – translates to 'my deep knowledge, if only I had you first'. Means, I wish I knew this beforehand.

Ston fílo sou min empistaftheís to mystikó sou o fílos ston fílo tha to pei kai eínai kakó de ko sou - translates to 'don't trust your secrets to your friends, as they will tell their friends, so it will come back to harm you'.

´E fíles eínai fídia - translates to 'the girlfriends are snakes' and means be careful who your friends are, because they might be the opposite.

Stou diaólou tin mána - translates 'to heck with your mother', but means that something is so far away that it is near the devil's mother.

΄Ο kalos o kapetánios sti fourtoúna faínetai - means that the good captain shows his skills when the going gets tough.

΄Ε koúnia pou se koúnage - translates to 'the swing that shook you', but means someone is telling you something that you don't believe. You're not saying they're lying, but you tease that they don't know what they're talking about!

Ta pollá lógia eínai ftohá - translates to 'many words are poor', but means do as I say and don't talk back.

΄Ola ta dáchtyla den eínai ta ídia - translates that 'not all my fingers are the same', but means that love is the same for all children, despite them all being different.

΄An den teriázame, den tha symbetheriázame - meaning if we weren't like-minded, our families wouldn't join by marriage.

῾O skýlos léei sti gáta kai i gáta stin ourá tou - the dog says to the cat and the cat to its tail.

῎Ena átomo pou fovátai ton thánato, pethaínei kathimeriná - a person who is afraid of death dies every day, so live for today and don't worry about tomorrow!

Pes mou pgíos énai o fílos sou, nas sou pó pgíos ésai - this one will likely be familiar to you as it means 'you are who your friends are'.

Ton gáidaro ekrývane kai faínontan ta aftiá tou - translates to 'the donkey was hidden and his ears were visible', meaning they were trying cover up the truth but it was obvious to everyone else.

To aíma neró den gínetai - blood doesn't become water, meaning family ties can't be broken.

῎Opou akoús polá kokória, argí na xymeróni – means where there are too many chiefs, results are delayed.

Me to dáskalo pou eheis, tétoia grámmata tha mátheis - means that the good teacher will teach you the best, or the other way around!

Horió pou faínetai kolaoúzo de théli - is a response you may get when you ask for someone's opinion and they respond by saying that no explanation is needed, as it's obvious that it is perfect or beautiful! Or, needs no broadcasting.

Ópou akoús pollá kerásia kráta kai mikró kaláthi - translates that 'when you hear that there are a lot of cherries, bring a small basket', but means don't believe what you hear as it's likely a huge exaggeration.

Opoíos katouráei sti thálassa, to vrískei sto aláti - means that whoever pees in the sea finds it in their table salt.

Dýo pódia den horáne se éna papoútsi - translates to 'two feet do not fit into one shoe', meaning that you are trying the impossible.

Tou poulioú to gála - translates to the 'bird's milk', but means that you'll try to do everything you can for someone out of love.

CHAPTER 3

~ "Yiayia-isms" ~

Tha fas xílo! - is up there on our laugh-out-loud list as it translates to 'you're going to eat wood!', but means that you're in a lot of trouble!

Na se vráso - translates to 'I'm going to boil you', but means that you're in big trouble!

Tha se fáo - translates to 'I'm going to eat you', but means that you're in big trouble!

Óti gyalízei den eínai hrysós – Not everything that shines is gold.

Alímono sou - means that if you don't do this right, there will be trouble.

Dáskale pou dídaskes kai nómo den ékratis - preaching the right thing to do but not actually doing it.

Άnthropos agrámmatos xýlo apelékito - means that whoever doesn't go to school, is as uneducated as a piece of wood that hasn't yet been shaped by a carpenter.

Έ kakí eínai sti fylakí - translates to 'the bad guys are in jail'.

Όpoíos den éhei myaló éhei pódia - those that don't use their brain/head walk around aimlessly.

Me énan sbáro dýo trigónia - means to kill two birds with one stone.

Kállio pénde kai sto héri, pará déka kai kartéti - translates to 'it's better to take the five and wait for the other five', meaning that if someone wants to only pay you half of what they owe you, it's best to take it and hope the rest will come!

Ό pséftis kai o kléftis ton proto hróno haírontai - translates to 'the liar and the thief rejoice in the first year', meaning that if you lie and cheat, you will eventually get caught.

Έrthan ta apaitoúmena na dióxoun ta kathoúmena - translates to 'the demands came to expel the accused', but means that the trouble-makers are chasing away the quiet ones.

Όpoíos thélei ta pollá hánei kai ta líga - translates to 'whoever wants the many, loses the few', meaning he who is greedy is likely to end up with the least.

Káthe pérsi kai kalýtera - meaning that the past year was better than this one.

Pan métron, áriston – moderation.

Kalýtera na se geláne pará na se klaíne - translates to 'it is better to laugh than to cry'. Meaning when you tell yourself it's okay to have someone tease you, but it's not okay when they talk behind your back to make you cry.

Akómi den vyikés apó to avgó - means that you haven't even come out of your egg yet! Or, you are not mature.

Káne to kaló kai ríxto sto gyaló - translates to 'do good and throw it in the water (ocean)', but means do something good but don't brag about it. Or, don't tell the right hand what the left hand is doing.

To den boró kai to de xéro kai ti kalá porévo - translates to 'I am not capable, and I do not know, and I don't want to get involved', and is the response that you would give to someone who is asking you to do something when you don't want to. Saying I cannot and don't know serves me well.

Eínai kalýtera na xéreis pará na éheis - translates to 'it's better to have knowledge than to have material objects' and means that knowledge is better than wealth.

Ta pollá logia eínai ftóheia - translates that 'too many words are poor', but means 'silence is golden' when someone is bragging too much.

Káthe empódio yia kaló - every obstacle is for the good.

To siganó potámi na fovásai - translates to 'be afraid of the slow river', but means to be careful of those who are quiet and soft-spoken.

Tréhei kai den ftánei - translates that 'you're running around so will never arrive', meaning there is so much to do but things will never get done.

Tis nýchtas e douliá, tin vlépi eméra kai gelláei! – translates to 'the night's work sees the day and laughs', and means that sometimes you're so busy that you don't realize you've made mistakes until the following morning, with fresh eyes.

Apó mikró kai apó treló mathaíneis tin alítheia - translates to 'from the young child and the mentally unstable person you learn the truth', and means that you can't hide a secret.

To gouroúni kai an to pléneis to sapoúni sou halás - if you wash the pig, your soap will spoil.

Ό kósmos tó éhi toúbano kai esí krýfo kamári - translates to 'the world is all drumming and we hide our pride', but means that everyone knows your secret and is talking about it.

E kóta ótan píni neró vlépi kai tón ouranó – translates to 'even the chickens look up at the sky when they drink water to give thanks to God', meaning be grateful and thankful for all you have.

Káne kaló yia na deis kaló - do good, to see good. But don't talk about it! Be humble.

Kemáte órthios – means that you're sleeping on your feet. Or, you're a moron!

Έ glóssa mou tha vgálei malliá - translates to 'my tongue will grow hair from all the yelling', but means you're tired of saying the same thing.

Ekeí pou eísai ímouna - edó pou eímai tha értheis - means that where I am now, you will arrive one day.

Tha myríso ta nýhia mou - translates to 'I will smell my nails', and means that I have no idea.

῾Osa de ftánei e alepoú ta kánei kremastária - translates to 'what the fox cannot reach, it pretends to save for later', but means that he doesn't admit something due to his inabilities, or that he didn't want to admit that he wasn't capable so would leave it for now.

E kamilá den ídie tin kaboúra tis, ídie to paidoú tis - translates to 'the camel didn't see her own hump, but sees her child's'. It means that we don't see, or we choose to overlook, our own flaws. But, instead, we are quick to point out those of others.

῾Eheis glóssa pandófla - translates to 'your tongue is as dirty as your slipper', but means you're talking too much.

Ama den éheis palió den éheis kai kanóurio - if you don't have old, you have no new.

Ipno elafrí kai onira gliká – translates to, 'have a nice calm sleep and sweets dreams'.

CHAPTER 4

~ Superstitions ~

Don't wash clothes on new year's day.

Trity kai dekatreís – means it's a Tuesday and the 13th so never plan a celebration on this day, as it will rain.

Place *Kouféta* (candy covered almonds) from a wedding under your pillow for three nights. You will marry who you dream of. For couples, place them under your pillow from a baptism, so you will be fertile.

In some areas of Greece, brides will write the names of all their single friends on the bottom of their shoes. Names that have been worn off by the end of the night are those that are said will get married in the near future.

Don't change bedsheets or clean the house until overnight guests that are departing have arrived at their final destination.

Always have your eyes open, and your legs closed!

Always exit the same door you have entered.

Don't whistle, or you'll get big boobs!

Never run after a bus, a ringing telephone, or a man!

Always make the sign of a cross on the outside of the aircraft just before you enter it… with your right foot first, of course.

If people are looking at or talking to you from afar, and you suspect that you might get *"máti"*, (the evil eye) scratch your bum and whisper under your breath "as much as you're giving is how much you will get", added with *"skórdo na fas"* or "eat garlic"!

Jumping (up to nine times) over a bonfire brings good luck.

Before departing on a long road trip, always cross yourself before you depart.

Always throw coins on the floorboards of someone's new car.

Don't chew gum late at night because it's like chewing dead people's bones!

Eat the crusts from your bread so that your mother-in-law will like you!

If you eat your meal right from the pot on the stove, it will rain on your wedding day.

Never place a loaf of bread upside down!

Make the sign of the cross over a loaf of bread before slicing it. Greeks believe that bread is a gift from God.

Bless whatever food you put in the oven, so it comes out just right.

Don't ask to "cheer" or do a toast with coffee as it is bad luck.

Don't stretch at the table as you will send your food down to the devil!

During the 12-days of Christmas, throw *loukoumádes* (Greek donut balls) on the roof so that the *kalikántzari (*goblins/gnomes) that come out at night to cause mischief become busy eating them and will stop cutting down the "world tree".

Place a knife on the counter or table, rather than handing it to someone directly.

When making *Avgoleméno* (chicken and egg soup), make a kissing sound with your lips while you pour the eggs into the warm soup so it will taste yummy.

Salt thrown behind the backs of visitors that have over-stayed their welcome will send them on their way!

Never share the same bar of soap, or you will have a fight with each other!

Salt sprinkled throughout a new home will ward off evil spirits.

When gifting a wallet or a purse, always put money inside for good luck.

Never sit on a kitchen table or counter!

Don't shake out the tablecloth at night.

Don't leave your purse on the floor, or all the money will leave you.

Never take bread, eggs or salt out of the house after the sun sets, or you and your family will risk being the receivers of the evil eye, or *"máti"*.

If you want to have children, do not leave your shoes upside down when sleeping!

If someone has a broom, make certain to move out of their way. If they touch you with it, they will sweep your life away!

Never step over anyone that's lying on the floor. If they're children, they won't grow. If they're adults, it'll send them to their grave early!

Don't whistle in the house or you'll invite evil spirits in.

Don't look at a mirror in the dark, as you will see the devil.

Chewing gum anytime at night has to be spit out because evil spirits will awaken and come after you.

Don't leave your clothes inside out, or your life will turn upside down!

Drawers or cabinet doors left open will invite people to gossip about you.

Placing cactus plants outside doorways will keep evil spirits out of your home!

When coming home from the hospital, touch steel or step on iron with the wish that you will become as strong as iron or *"sederenios"* and will heal quickly.

When you sneeze, someone is apparently talking about you, or thinking of you.

When walking along the street, if you can't avoid running into a priest whisper *"skórdo"* (garlic) to avoid any bad omens!

Restrain from having your shoes lying on their side, as it will bring much bad luck, or even death!

Put your hair up when you sleep or you'll get a hairy face!

Don't cut bangs or you'll grow hair on your forehead!

Don't wash your hair on Sunday if you want to be productive throughout the next week!

Don't cut your nails on a Wednesday or Friday.

Men are the head of the households; however, women are the necks that tell the head which way to turn!

Don't cut ribbons off your wedding or shower gifts, or you won't be able to have children.

Never give knives as wedding gifts as it will cut the marriage apart!

Never give soap as a gift, otherwise you will start a fight with that person.

If you must give soap, include a coin or a small amount of money to ward off any evil vibes!

Like soap, giving perfume is another gift that's sure to ruin any relationship.

God bless every Yiayia and Pappou, and may all their sayings live on through all of us for generations to come!

"GREEK-LISH"

Tirokeki	Cheesecake
Barbarquera	BBQ grill
Roofianos	Roofer
Carpeto	Carpet
Carro	Car
Hotdogia	Hotdogs
Passahport	Passport

Key Word Index

If you would like to be a part of a future edition of this book, by contributing (with credit) sayings, proverbs, or advice, please email angevardalos@gmail.com.

All submissions will be gratefully considered. Thank you!

You can be part of the conversation on social media—on Instagram **@cheerswithAnge** or **@yiayiaapproved_book**, and the **YIAYIA APPROVED** group page on Facebook.

ABOUT THE AUTHOR

Angela Vardalos was born in Winnipeg, Manitoba, Canada, taking her husband's name Saclamacis when they married in 1988. After three years, they moved to Toronto where she held a series of corporate positions in Marketing, Corporate Communications & Public Relations, retiring in 2021. Angela currently lives in Calgary, Alberta, Canada, along with her husband Jim and their two daughters. She enjoys long hikes in the Rocky Mountains, is addicted to baking sourdough bread, loves Pilates, travelling, and drinking bubbles.

Made in the USA
Middletown, DE
13 January 2022

58624322R00033